JavaScript

A Guide to Learning the JavaScript Programming Language

Troy Dimes

Contents

Your Free Gift

As a thank you for reading this book, I would like to give you a free copy of "Common Coding Problems Solved Using JavaScript." It's a perfect complement to this book and will help you along your JavaScript journey.

Visit http://www.linuxtrainingacademy.com/javascript-guide/ to download your free gift.

Introduction

JavaScript is a dynamic computer programming language that is commonly used in web browsers to control the behavior of web pages and interact with users. It allows for asynchronous communication and can update parts of a web page or even replace the entire content of a web page. You'll see JavaScript being used to display date and time information, perform animations on a web site, validate form input, suggest results as a user types into a search box, and more.

Even though JavaScript is by far the most popular client side programming language in use today, it can and is used on the server side as well. Node.js, Meteor, Wakanda, CouchDB, and MongoDB are just a few examples of where you'll find and be able to use JavaScript on the server side. The time you invest in learning JavaScript can be doubly rewarding as JavaScript keeps moving into more and more areas of computing.

No matter if you plan to use JavaScript on the client side in a web browser, on the server side, or both, you will need to learn the fundamentals of the language. That's what this book will give you. When you finish reading this book you will feel comfortable and confident programming in the JavaScript language.

What is JavaScript?

JavaScript is a client-side scripting language which is used for web browsers. It primarily focuses on helping developers to interact with the web page as well as the web browser itself. JavaScript is loosely based on the Java programming language. Even though it has a similar programming methodology and syntax, it cannot be considered a light version of Java. It is truly its own language that finds its home in web browsers all over the world and enables a magnified user experience in web applications and on web sites alike.

How JavaScript Can Be Used?

JavaScript is mainly a scripting language that can be used in HTML pages. JavaScript was originally called Live Script, but at the time of its release, Java had become very popular. Mainly for marketing reasons Netscape changed its name to "JavaScript" at the last moment and updated to be more Java-like. This is the reason which gave rise to the fact that JavaScript is a "dumbed-down" version of Java. But this is not at all true in reality. JavaScript cannot be strictly considered as a programming language. It is instead a scripting language since it uses the browser to do the dirty work. If you direct an image to be

3

replaced by another one, JavaScript asks the browser to perform it. Since it is the browser that actually does the work, you only require to pull some strings by writing some relatively simple lines of code. That's one reason JavaScript is a relatively easy language to start with.

However, JavaScript can be a bit difficult too. First, in spite of its simple appearance it is a full-fledged programming language and you can write quite complex and complicated programs in JavaScript. When dealing with client side web scripts this is not usually the case, but it's quite possible to write extremely complicated JavaScript code. This means that there are some complex programming structures that can be understood only after continued study.

The second and more important thing is that there are differences between web browsers. Even though all modern web browsers support JavaScript, there is no fixed law that states all of them have to support the exact same JavaScript. We can therefore say that it is easy to learn basic JavaScript but when it comes to writing advanced scripts it is very likely that browser differences will pop up.

On the client side, JavaScript has been developed to be used in a web browser in conjunction with HTML pages. This has certain security implications. When a user visits a JavaScript-enhanced web site, they request a certain HTML (web) page without knowing if it contains JavaScript or not. The HTML page is delivered to the browser, including the scripts. The scripts typically run automatically when the page is loaded or when the user takes some sort of action. Generally, the user can't do anything to stop the scripts. He can definitely turn off JavaScript, but only a few end users know how this can be done. An innocent user essentially downloads a random program and allows it to execute on his machine. To enhance security there are strict rules as to what this program can and cannot do. For example, it cannot read files from the file system or write them to the file system on the computer. Any other programs cannot be executed by JavaScript only. JavaScript is a client-side language for downloading a new HTML language or sending a mail. This means that it is not involved in any kind of connection to other computer. The hackers regularly find weakness in the Microsoft Explorer and add some file system commands in combination with its Active X Technology. Thus Internet Explorer is structurally less safe than other browsers. The first JavaScript virus worked in such a way.

JavaScript works on things that are in HTML pages or part of the browser. One cannot influence anything that's not contained by the browser. But there are some no–go areas even within the browser. JavaScript, basically, wants to protect the user's privacy by not allowing certain actions.

What You Will Learn in the Coming Chapters

In the first chapter you will learn how to configure your environment for programming in JavaScript. You will learn what tools or software are required, which web browser to use, recommended web browser plugins, text editors and some other related facts. The next chapter covers HTML, its basic structure, and where you must place JavaScript code in an HTML document. The third chapter will cover the use of variables and strings. Next you will learn about numbers and math and the various operations related to them such as addition, subtraction, multiplication, division, and more. You will also learn about the order of operations and how to use parenthesis to create your own order. Chapter five introduces booleans and conditionals and explains comparators and various methods to make decision in your programs. The sixth chapter covers functions including what they are, when to use them, how to define them, and how you can put them to good use. The seventh chapter is about arrays, loops and conditions. The final chapter explains what associative arrays are and when to use them.

Chapter 1: Configuring Your Environment for JavaScript Programming

To begin developing in JavaScript you will need a good working environment. In this chapter you will learn how to setup the programs you will need when writing code in JavaScript.

Source Code Editors

First off you will need a piece of software that you can use to write and edit your JavaScript programs. You can use what is called an IDE, which stands for Integrated Development Environment. There are several options to choose from, but two good features to have are syntax highlighting and autocompletion. If you already using a source code editor or IDE with another programming language, make sure that it supports JavaScript. Some may not support JavaScript at all while others will allow support to be added by installing an additional plugin. If you do not already have a source code editor that you like,

7

check out the following suggestions.

Free IDEs

Aptana - http://www.aptana.com

Eclipse - https://www.eclipse.org

NetBeans - https://netbeans.org

Spket IDE - http://www.spket.com

Commercial IDEs

Intellij Webstorm - https://www.jetbrains.com/webstorm

Komodo IDE - http://komodoide.com

MicroSoft Visual Studio - http://www.visualstudio.com

IntelliJ IDEA - https://www.jetbrains.com/idea

Lightweight Editors

Since web pages (HTML documents) and JavaScript code are simply plain text, you can skip using a full blown IDE and instead use a simple text editor. Here are a few for your consideration.

Windows

- Geany: http://www.geany.org/
- JEdit: http://www.jedit.org/
- Komodo Edit: http://komodoide.com/komodo-edit/

- Notepad++: http://notepad-plus-plus.org/
- SciTe: http://www.scintilla.org/SciTE.html

Mac

- JEdit: http://www.jedit.org/
- Komodo Edit: http://komodoide.com/komodo-edit/
- Sublime Text: http://www.sublimetext.com/
- TextWrangler: http://www.barebones.com/products/textwrangler/

Linux

- Emacs: https://www.gnu.org/software/emacs/
- Geany: http://www.geany.org/
- JEdit: http://www.jedit.org/
- Komodo Edit: http://komodoide.com/komodo-edit/
- Sublime Text: http://www.sublimetext.com/
- SciTe: http://www.scintilla.org/SciTE.html
- Vim: http://www.vim.org/

Web Browsers

You will need at least one web browser. The most popular web browsers are Firefox, Chrome, Safari, Opera, and Internet Explorer. If you want to ensure your JavaScript code works correctly in most enviornments, try it out in multiple web browsers.

Firefox: http://getfirefox.com

Chrome: http://www.google.com/chrome

Safari: http://support.apple.com/downloads/#safari

Opera: http://www.opera.com

Internet Explorer: http://windows.microsoft.com/en-us/internet-explorer

Web Browser Plugins

These plugins are optional and won't be necessary or covered in this book. However, they are listed here if you want to explore them on your own. They can help you write and debug JavaScript code.

Firebug: http://getfirebug.com

Firebug is a plugin for the Firefox web browser that provides a wide variety of developer tools including a JavaScript debugger and logger.

Firebug Lite: https://getfirebug.com/firebuglite

A stripped down version of the Firebug plugin for the Chrome web browser.

Chapter 2: HTML

HTML stands for Hypertext Markup Language. It is a markup language that tells a web browser how to display a web page. HTML documents are simply plain text files with special codes called tags that a web browser uses to interpret and display information to the screen. HTML files can have either a `.htm` or `.html` file extension. The `.html` file extension is more prevalent than `.htm` and that is what we will be using in throughout this book.

Open your favorite text editor and type the following text:

```
<html>
<head>
<title>My First Web Page</title>
</head>
<body>
This is my first web page. <b>This text is bold.</b>
</body>
```

```
</html>
```

Save the file as `mypage.html`. Start your Internet browser. Select Open (or Open Page) in the File menu of the browser. A dialog box will appear after this. Select Browse (or Choose File) for the HTML file location that you just created - `mypage.html` - select it and select Open. After this, you will see an address in the dialog box, like `C:\MyDocuments\mypage.html`. Click OK, and the page will be displayed by the browser.

What you just created is a skeleton HTML document. It is the minimum information that is required for a web document and all web documents must contain these basic components. This document, like all other HTML documents, contains a series of tags. HTML tags come in the format of a less-than sign (<) followed by a character or a word. Next the tag can contain additional text, but every tag will end in a greater-than sign (>).

The first tag in the HTML document is <html>. This tag tells your browser that it is the start of an HTML document. The last tag in your document is </html> and it tells the browser that this is the end of the HTML document. The text between the <head> tag and the </head> tag is the header information. This information is not displayed in the main browser window. The text between the <title> tags is the title of the document. It is used to uniquely identify each document and is displayed in the browser window's title bar. The text between the <body>

tags is the text that is displayed in your browser. The text between the <b> and </b> tags will be displayed in a bold font.

You should start to notice a pattern. For each opening tag there is a closing tag. For example, <title> is the opening tag for the title of the page and </title> is the closing tag. Notice that the closing tag includes a forward slash (/) after the less-than sign (<).

How to View HTML Source

The best way to learn HTML is to look at how other people have coded their HTML pages. For this, simply select the View menu in your browser's toolbar and click on "View Source" or "View Page Source." This opens a window that will show you the actual HTML source code of the page. Practice now by viewing the source of the HTML for the page you just created.

HTML Tags

HTML tags are used for marking-up HTML elements. They are surrounded by the two characters < and >. The surrounding characters are known as angle brackets. They normally come in pairs like <b> and </b> .The first tag in a pair being the start tag and the second one is the end tag. The text between the start and end tags is the element content. These tags are not case sensitive which means that <b> is the same as <B>.

Logical vs. Physical Tags

There are both logical tags and physical tags in HTML. Logical tags are the ones designed to describe to the browser the enclosed text's meaning. One example is the `<strong>` `</strong>` tag. When you place text in between these tags you are actually hinting to the browser that the text is of greater importance. All browsers by default make the text appear bold when in between the `<strong>` and `</strong>` tags.

Physical tags, on the other hand, provide specific instructions on how to display the text they are enclosing.

Examples of physical tags include:

> `<b>`: used for making the text bold.
> `<big>`: used for making the text mostly one size bigger than what's around it.
> `<i>`: used for making the text italic.

If we look at the previous HTML example on previous page, this is an HTML element:

```
<b>This text is bold.</b>
```

The HTML element starts with a start tag: `<b>`
The above element contains a string: "This text is bold."
The string ends with a closing tag: `</b>`
The tag "`<b>` `</b>`" means that the string in between these will be displayed as bold.
Another HTML is the `<body>` tag. Code for a web page starts with a start tag of `<body>` and ends with the ending tag of

</body>. The <body> tag's purpose is to define the HTML element that contains the HTML document's body.

Nested Tags

In the example above you may have noticed the <body> tag also contains other tags, such as the <b> tag. While enclosing an element within multiple tags, the tag that is opened the last should be the first to be closed.

For example:

```
<p><b><em>This is NOT the correct way of closing
nested tags.</p></em></b>
<p><b><em>This IS the correct way of closing nested
tags.</em></b></p>
```

Why Use Lowercase Tags?

You may notice we've used lowercase tags even though I said that HTML tags are not case sensitive. In HTML, <B> means the exact same thing as <b>. The World Wide Web Consortium (W3C), the group responsible for developing web standards, recommends lowercase tags and tag attributes in their HTML 4 recommendation.

Tags can have attributes. These provide additional information about the HTML elements on the page. A <tag> tells the browser to do something, whereas an attribute tells the browser *how* to do it. For example, when we add the `bgcolor` attribute, we can inform the browser that the background color of the page must be blue, like this: `<body bgcolor="blue">`. This defines an HTML table: `<table>`. You can tell the browser that the table must have no borders by using an attribute like so: `<table border="0">`.

Attributes always come in name/value pairs like: name="value". Their values must always be enclosed in quotes. The most common are the double style quotes, but single style quotes are also allowed. In some situations, for example when the attribute value itself contains quotes, it is required to use single quotes: sentence = ' She said, "This is fun," even though she is just starting to code.'

Basic HTML Tags

The most important tags in HTML are those that define headings, line breaks and paragraphs.

`<html>` Defines an HTML document
`<body>` Defines the document's body
`<h1>` to `<h6>` Defines header 1 to header 6
`<p>` Defines a paragraph
`<br>` Inserts a single line break
`<hr>` Defines a horizontal rule
`<!-->` Defines a comment

Headings

They are defined with the <h1> to <h6> tags. The <h1> tag defines the largest heading where as the <h6> tag defines the smallest. An extra blank line is automatically added by HTML before and after a heading. Align is a useful heading attribute

```
<h5 align="left">You can align headings.</h5>
<h5 align="center">This is a centered heading.</h5>
<h5  align="right">This  is  a  heading  aligned  to  the
right.</h5>
```

Paragraphs

Paragraphs are defined with the <p> tag. You may think of a paragraph as a text block. You may use the align attribute with a paragraph tag as well.

```
<p align="left">This is a paragraph</p>
<p align="center">this is another paragraph</p>
```

Try the following code for practice:

```
<html>
<head>
<title>My Second Web Page</title>
</head>
<body>
<h1 align="center">My Second Web Page</h1>
<p>Welcome to my second web page.</p>
<p>After learning HTML, I will be able to create web
pages like an expert.</p>
</body>
</html>
```

Save the page as mypage2.html and open the file in your web browser.

Placing JavaScript in an HTML Document

The `<SCRIPT>` tag lets the browser know that JavaScript code follows. It is typically embedded in the HTML.

```
<SCRIPT language = "JavaScript">
// JavaScript code goes here
</SCRIPT>
```

The JavaScript Code is placed below the `<HTML>` TML tag and above the `<BODY>` tag in an HTML body.

```
<html>
<head>
<script type="text/javascript">
...
</script>
</head>
<body>
<script type="text/javascript">
...
</script>
</body>
</html>
```

Chapter 3: Variables and Strings

Variables

Variables in JavaScript are defined by using the 'var' operator, which is short for *variable*. It is then followed by the variable name. Here's an example:

```
var test = "hi";
```

Here, the variable `test` is declared and given an initialization value of `"hi"`, which is a string. Since the JavaScript programming language is loosely typed, the interpreter automatically creates a string value for `test` without any explicit type declaration. Two or more variables can also be defined using the same `var` statement.

```
var test = "hi", test2 = "hello";
```

The given code defines the variable `test` to a value of `"hi"` and the variable `test2` to a value of `"hello"`. Variables that use the same `var` statement need not be of the same type but they can be different as the following example.

```
var test = "hi", age = 25;
```

This example defines `test` in addition to another variable named `age` that has the value of `25`. Even if `test` and `age` are two different data types, it is totally legal in JavaScript. Variables in JavaScript do not require initialization because they are actually initialized behind the scenes. Therefore, this line of code is valid:

```
var test;
```

Unlike Java, variables can hold different values at different times. This is an advantage of variables that are loosely typed. You can initialize a variable with a string value and later on set it to a number value, like this:

```
var test = "hi";
alert(test); //outputs "hi"
//do something else here
test = 55;
alert(test); //outputs "55"
```

The above code will output both the string and the number values without incident. However, it's a best coding practice to use the same data type throughout your program for a given variable.

For variables names, a name must adhere tp the following simple rules:

The first character should be a letter, a dollar sign ($), or an an underscore (_)

All other characters can be underscores, alphanumeric characters or dollar signs

All these variable names are legal:

```
var test;
var $test;
var $1;
var _$te$t2;
```

Just because the variable names are syntactically correct does not mean that you should use them. Variables should stick to one of the well-known naming conventions:

Camel Notation — In this notation, the first letter is lowercase and each appended word begins with an uppercase letter. This is sometimes called CamelCase. Here's an example.

```
var myTestValue = 0, mySecondTestValue = "hi";
```

Pascal Notation —the first letter is uppercase and each appended word begins with an uppercase letter. For example:

```
var MyTestValue = 0, MySecondTestValue = "hi";
```

Hungarian Type Notation — This notation prepends a lowercase letter to the beginning of a Pascal Notation variable name to indicate which type of variable.

To clarify, `i` means integer and `s` means string in the following line of JavaScript.

```
var iMyTestValue = 0, sMySecondTestValue = "hi";
```

The table below lists prefixes for defining JavaScript variables with Hungarian Type Notation.

23

Type	Prefix	Example
Array	a	aValues
Boolean	b	bFound
Float (Number)	f	fValue
Function	fn	fnMethod
Integer (Number)	i	iValue
Object	o	oType
Regular Expression	re	rePattern
String	s	sValue
Variant (can be any type)	v	vValue

Getting Input from the User

In the following code, the `sayHi()` method has been called before any text is displayed on the page, which means that the alert will pop up before the text "This is the beginning of the text on the page." But you should know that this method of calling JavaScript inside the `<body>` of a page is not recommended and should be avoided almost every single time when programming in JavaScript. Event handlers should be employed for using JavaScript in the body of a page.

```
<html>
<head>
<title>Title of Page</title>
<script language="JavaScript">
function sayHi() {
    alert("Hi");
}
</script>
</head>
<body>
  <script type="text/javascript">
     sayHi();
  </script>
  This is the beginning of the text on the page.
</body>
</html>
```

Displaying Text in the Web Browser and on the Screen

In JavaScript you can display output in the web browser by "writing" to the HTML document. The format is `document.write()`. You can place the output you want to display within the parenthesis. If it's simply text you want to display, wrap the text in quotation marks. If you are displaying the contents of a variable, use the variable name. Here's an example that will cause "Hello there!" to be displayed in the web browser.

```
<html>
<head>
<script language="JavaScript">
```

```
document.write('Hello there!');
</script>
</head>
</html>
```

This example results in the same output, however a variable is used.

```
<html>
<head>
<script language="JavaScript">
var greeting = 'Hello there!';
document.write(greeting);
</script>
</head>
</html>
```

Concatenation

The concatenate method is used to concatenate, or combine, one or more strings to the primitive value of the String object. In this method, a string primitive value is returned as a result and leaves the original String object intact:

```
var oStringObject = new String("hello ");
var sResult = oStringObject.concat("world");
alert(sResult); //outputs "hello world"
```

```
alert(oStringObject); //outputs "hello "
```

Calling the `concat()` method in the previous code will give the
result "hello world", while the String object contents remains
"hello ". Therefore, using the addition operator (+) to
concatenate strings is much more common because it logically
indicates the actual behavior.

```
var oStringObject = new String("hello ");
var sResult = oStringObject + "world";
alert(sResult); //outputs "hello world"
alert(oStringObject); //outputs "hello "
```

What if you are not sure if a character exists or not in a particular
string? That's where the `indexOf()` and `lastIndexOf()`
find their use. The `indexOf()` and `lastIndexOf()`
methods have the function of returning the position of a
substring within another string . The difference between both of
them is that the `indexOf()` method starts looking for the
substring at the start of the string (character 0) while the
`lastIndexOf()` method starts looking for the substring at
the end of the string. For example:

```
var oStringObject = new String("hello world");
alert(oStringObject.indexOf("o")); //outputs "4"
alert(oStringObject.lastIndexOf("o")); //outputs "7"
```

The first occurrence of the string "o" takes place at position 4, which is the "o" in "hello" whereas the last occurrence of the string "o" is in the word "world" at position 7. `indexOf()` and `lastIndexOf()` return the same position if there is only one occurrence of "o"in the string.

Comments in JavaScript

Comments are for the benefit of those writing and reading source code. JavaScript will simply ignore any comments it encounters. This gives you a way to explain your code. You can use comments to summarize what is going on in a complex section of code. Comments are great if someone needs to look at the code long after it was written. You might remember what your intention was when writing the code, but may forget over time.

In JavaScript, a single line comment is prefixed with two forward slashes (//).

```
// This is a comment.  JavaScript ignores comments.
```

You can comment part of a line like so:

```
var name;  // This will hold the user's name.
```

You can chain multiple single line comments together.

```
// The following code:
//      Computes the hosting costs for one server.
//      Returns the hosting cost for one server.
```

You can also create multi-line comments. Start a multi-line comment with a forward slash followed by an asterisk (/*). End a multi-line comment with an asterisk followed by a forward slash (*/). Anything that comes between /* and */ is a comment.

```
/* """ This is the start of the comment.
This is another line.
This is the last line in the comment. */
```

Here's another example.

```
/*
I've started this comment down here.
JavaScript will not try to interpret these lines
since they are comments.
*/
```

You can even create a single line quote using the multi-line quote syntax.

```
/* This is a comment.  Comments are fun. */
```

Chapter 4: Numbers and Math

JavaScript can support several operations with numbers. The following table lists the most commonly used numeric operations.

Symbol	Operation
+	add
-	subtract
*	multiply
/	divide
%	modulo

Addition Operator (+)

The add operator performs the operation of finding the sum of numeric operands or string concatenation.

Syntax: x + y

Examples:

```
// Number + Number -> addition
1 + 2 // 3

// Boolean + Number -> addition
true + 1 // 2

// Boolean + Boolean -> addition
false + false // 0

// Number + String -> concatenation
5 + "foo" // "5foo"

// String + Boolean -> concatenation
"foo" + false // "foofalse"

// String + String -> concatenation
"foo" + "bar" // "foobar"
```

Subtraction Operator

The subtraction operator performs the function of subtracting the two operands, giving their difference.

Syntax: x - y

Examples:

```
5 - 3      // 2
3 - 5      // -2
"foo" - 3 // NaN (Not a number.)
```

Note that in JavaScript, NaN means "not a number."

Division Operator

The division operator produces the quotient of its operands. The right operand is the divisor and the left operand is the dividend.

Syntax: x / y

Examples:

```
1 / 2        // returns 0.5 in JavaScript
1 / 2        // returns 0 in Java
// (none of the numbers is explicitly a floating
point number)
1.0 / 2.0   // returns 0.5 in both JavaScript and Java
2.0 / 0     // returns Infinity in JavaScript
2.0 / 0.0   // returns Infinity too
2.0 / -0.0 // returns -Infinity in JavaScript
```

Multiplication Operator

This operator performs the product of the operands.

Syntax: x * y

Examples:

```
2 * 2 // 4
-2 * 2 // -4
Infinity * 0 // NaN
Infinity * Infinity // Infinity
"foo" * 2 // NaN
```

Modulus Operator

It is used for calculating the remainder of two values when they were divided. The modulus operator produces the remainder value only and is very useful for seeing whether the values are divisible by a specified number.

Syntax: x % y

Examples:

```
12 % 5 // 2
-1 % 2 // -1
NaN % 2 // NaN
```

Order of Operations

The examples that we have looked at so far involve one

operation. But many times when we perform operations, we need to incorporate different operations together into a single command. This may result in several possible results depending on the order in which the operations are performed. JavaScript always uses the same rules to work out which order to calculate things in.

• ++variable and --variable are performed first because having the operator in front indicates that we want to add or subtract one before using the result in the subsequent calculation.
• Division, Multiplication and taking remainders are performed next, moving left to right.
• After this, addition and subtraction are performed also moving from the left.
• The variable++ and variable-- operations are performed last so that we use the original values that the variables have in the calculations before the value in the variable itself is changed.

If we want to force an addition or subtraction to take place before the multiplications and divisions then we have to to place that calculation inside of parentheses. Anything in parentheses is done before any multiplications and divisions.
Here are some examples. I have put the answers on the right which will enable you to see what result JavaScript would produce were it to perform these calculations.

a $5 + 3 * 6 = 23$

b $4 * 7 / 2 + 3 = 17$

c $17 \% 3 + 22 * 5 = 112$

d   (5 + 3) * 6 = 48

e   4 * 7 / (2 + 3) = 5.6

With (a) the multiplication is performed before the addition and so the result is twenty three.

In (b) we multiply the four and seven together first and then divide by two to give fourteen to which three is finally added.

Example (c) takes the remainder from dividing seventeen by three. Three goes five times into seventeen with two left over. This means that 17%3 equals 2. After this, twenty two and five are multiplied together to give 110. The results of these two intermediate calculations are added together to give a final answer.

Examples (d) and (e) show how you can modify the first two examples forcing JavaScript to perform the additions first.

Exercise

Write an program that performs addition, subtraction, multiplication and remainder (modulus) of two numbers.

Solution

```
<html>
<head>
        <title>Operators</title>
        <script>
                var num1 = 34;
                var num2 = 74;
                total = num1 + num2;
                document.write(total);
        </script>
</head>
<body>
</body>
</html>
```

Chapter 5: Booleans and Conditionals

A Boolean is a value that is either true or false. You can think of boolean as a binary value. IE, it is either off, zero, or on, one. Booleans are also great for situations where yes/no type of answers or data needs to be tracked.

JavaScript has a Boolean() function. It's used to determine if a statement is true or false. Let's look at a couple of examples.

```
itIsTrue = Boolean(true);    // True
itIsFalse = Boolean(false);  // False
```

In the previous examples the values were explicitly set to true and false. However, the Boolean() function can evaluate the truth of an expression as in the following examples.

```
itIsTrue = new Boolean(10 > 2);      // True
itIsFalse = new Boolean(10 > 200);   // False
```

The isItTrue value ends up being true since the Boolean()
function evaluated the statement 10 > 2 and determined that it
indeed was true. Likewise 10 is not greater than 200, so itIsFalse
holds the boolean value of False.

The Boolean() function returns true for anything that has a value.
All these statements are true.

```
Boolean(1);
Boolean('Hello!');
Boolean(5551231234);
Boolean(-99.9);
Boolean('This is true!');
```

The Boolean() function returns false for anything that does not
have a real value. This includes zero, NaN (not a number), and
empty strings. These are all false.

```
Boolean(0);
Boolean(-0);
Boolean("");
Boolean(NaN);
```

A Boolean object should not be used to convert a non-boolean value to a boolean value. Use the Boolean() function to perform this type of task. Said in another way, do not include the new keyword before the boolean function when creating variables.

```
x = Boolean(expression);      // Do this.
x = new Boolean(expression); // Do NOT do this.
```

Comparators

Comparators are used to compare two values. Comparators return a value of true or false, a boolean. Here are different type of comparators.

Comparison Operator (===)

Comparison operators are those which are used in logical statements to find equality or difference between values or variables.

Not Equal Operator (!==)

!== means the variables are not equal and do not have equal type.

Greater Than Operator (>)

This operator is used for comparing the two values. This operator means greater then or when vise-versaly used is called smaller then.

If statement

It is used when we want something is to be checked first and if the check statement is true then only the furher code is executed . You can use the if statement to specify a JavaScript code block to be executed if a condition is true.

Syntax:

```
if (some_condition) {
    // This code block will get executed
    // if some_condition is true.
}
```

Example:

Set the variable "greeting" to be "It is light outside" if time is less than 18:00.

```
if (time < 18) {
    greeting = "It is light outside";
}
```

if-else

We use the if else statement to add an additional check. This additional check will get evaluated if the first condition is false.

Syntax:

```
if (first_condition) {
    // This code block will get executed
    // if first_condition is true.
} else if (second_condition) {
    // This code block will get executed
    // if first_condition is false and
    //   second_condition is true.
} else {
    // This code block will get executed
    // if first_condition and second_condition are
    // both false
}
```

Example:

If the variable age is greater than 65, then the age_class variable will be set to "elderly." If that is false, then age > 34 gets evaluated. If that is true, the age_class is set to middle aged. If that is false, then age > 17 gets evaluated. If that is true, then age_class is set to "Adult." Finally, if all those conditions evaluate to false then age_class is set to "Child."

Age: Age Class

65+: Elderly

35 – 64: Middle aged

18 – 34: Adult

0 – 17: Child

```
if (age > 65) {
    age_class = "Elderly";
} else if (age > 34) {
    age_class = "Middle aged";
} else if (age > 17) {
    age_class = "Adult";
} else {
    age_class = "Child";
}
```

if-else-if

The if-else-if statement works on very similar logic. It will first check for the first comparison and will proceed accordingly. If the first statement is false it moves to the "else" part of the code. Under the else code is again an "if" statement and the entire procedure is repeated again till we have an output.

Syntax:

```
if (expression) {
    code block;
} else {
    if (expression) {
        code block;
    }
}
```

switch

The switch statement is used to select one of the many code blocks that are to be executed.

Syntax:

```
switch (expression) {
    case n:
        code block
        break;
    case n:
        code block
        break;
    default:
    default code block
}
```

This is how the switch statement works:

The switch expression is calculated only once. The expression's value is compared with the values of each case. If a match is found, the code block associated with that case is executed.

Example:

Use today's weekday number to calculate weekday name. We'll assume that Sunday = 1, Monday=2, Tuesday=3, etc.

```
switch (new Date().getDay()) {
    case 0:
```

```
        today = "Sunday";
        break;
    case 1:
        today = "Monday";
        break;
    case 2:
        today = "Tuesday";
        break;
    case 3:
        today = "Wednesday";
        break;
    case 4:
        today = "Thursday";
        break;
    case 5:
        today = "Friday";
        break;
    case 6:
        today = "Saturday";
        break;
}
```

Exercise:

Write some JavaScript code to let a person know if he or she is old enough to vote. Assume that the minimal voting age is 18.

Solution:

```html
<html>
<head>
    <title>Can You Vote?</title>
</head>

<body>
    <p>Input your age and click the button:</p>

    <form>
        <input id="age" value="18">
        <button onclick="myFunction()">Click</button>
    </form>

    <p id="demo"></p>
    <script>
    function myFunction() {
      var age,voteable;
      age = document.getElementById("age").value;
      voteable = (age < 18) ? "Too young":"Old enough";
      document.getElementById("demo").innerHTML = voteable + " to vote.";
    }
    </script>
</body>
</html>
```

Chapter 6: Functions

A function is a group of reusable code that can be called anywhere in the program. This removes the need of writing same code again and again. It helps programmers to write modular code. A big program can be divided in a number of small and manageable functions. JavaScript also supports all the features necessary to write modular code using functions.

Function Definition

Before a function is used we need to define that function. The best way for defining a function in JavaScript is to use the function keyword, followed by a unique function name and a list of parameters, and a statement block that is surrounded by curly braces. The basic syntax is:

```
<script type="text/Javascript">
<!--
function   function_name(parameter_list) {
        statements
}
//-->
</script>
```

Example:

A simple function taking no parameters called sayHello is defined
as:

```
<script type="text/Javascript">
<!--
function sayHello() {
    alert("Hello there");
}
//-->
</script>
```

Function Parameters

We have learned function without parameters. There is a facility
for passing different parameters when we call a function. These
parameters that are passed can be captured inside the function
and can be manipulated as per requirement. Multiple
parameters can be taken by a function which is separated by
comma.

Example:

Let us modify our *sayHello* function. It will take two parameters this time:

```
<script type="text/Javascript">
<!--
function sayHello(name, age) {
    alert(name + " is " + age + " years old.");
}
//-->
</script>
```

Note: We have used + operator to concatenate string and number. JavaScript does not mind to add numbers into strings.

We can call this function as follows:

```
<script type="text/Javascript">
<!--
        sayHello('Sarah', 7 );
//-->
</script>
```

Calling a Function

You would require to write the name of that function To invoke a function somewhere later in the script which is as follows:

```
<script type="text/Javascript">
<!--
        sayHello();
//-->
</script>
```

We define a JavaScript function with the function keyword which is followed by a name and then followed by parentheses ().

Function names may contain, underscores, digits and dollar signs, letters (same rules as variables).

The parentheses can include parameter names which are separated by commas: (parameter1, parameter2, ...)

The code which the function will execute is placed inside curly brackets: {}

```
functionName(parameter1, parameter2, parameter3) {
    code to be executed
}
```

Function parameters are the names that are listed in the definition of function . Function arguments are the real values which are received by the function when we invoke it. The arguments are used as local variables inside the function.

The code in the function is executed when "something" calls the function:

- When a user clicks a button

- When it is called from JavaScript code

- Self invoked

When a return statement is reached by a JavaScript, the function will stop executing. If the function was called from a statement, JavaScript will "return" to execute the code after the calling statement.

Functions mostly compute a value. This value is "returned" back to the "caller."

Example

Calculating the product of two numbers, and returning the result:

```
var x = myFunction(4, 3); // Function is called,
                          // return value will be x
function myFunction(a, b) {
    return a * b; // Function returns the product of
                  // a and b
}
```

The result of x will be:

12

Also note that functions are objects in Javascript.

Arguments
The arguments object is an Array-like object corresponding to the arguments passed to a function. The arguments object is a

local variable that is available within all functions.

By using the arguments object we can refer to a function's arguments within the function. This object will contain an entry for each argument that is passed to the function, the first entry's index starting at 0. If a function is passed three arguments, you can refer to the argument as given below:

```
arguments[0]
arguments[1]
arguments[2]
```

The arguments can also be set:

```
arguments[1] = 'new value';
```

The arguments object is similar to an Array, but does not have any properties of arrays except length. It does not have the pop method for example. However you can be convert in into a real Array:

```
var args = Array.prototype.slice.call(arguments);
```

One must not slice on arguments since it prevents optimizations in JavaScript engines such as V8.

If Array generics are available, you can use the following instead:

```
var args = Array.slice(arguments);
```

The arguments object can be available only within a function body. If you attempt to access the arguments object outside of a function declaration, it will result in an error.

You may use the arguments object if you want to call a function with more arguments than it is formally declared to accept. This is useful for functions that may be passed a variable number of arguments. You can use arguments.length to find the number of arguments that will be passed to the function, and then process each argument by using the arguments object.

This is an example of defining a function that concatenates several strings. The function is defined as follows:

```
function myConcat(separator) {
    var args = Array.prototype.slice.call(arguments,
1);
    return args.join(separator);
}
```

Any number of arguments can be passed to this function, and it creates a list using each argument as an item in the list.

```
// returns "red, orange, blue"
myConcat(", ", "red", "orange", "blue");
// returns "elephant; giraffe; lion; cheetah"
```

```
myConcat(";    ",    "elephant",    "giraffe",    "lion",
"cheetah");
// returns "sage. basil. oregano. pepper. parsley"
myConcat(". ", "sage", "basil", "oregano", "pepper",
"parsley");
```

This example displays a clock in the web browser.

```
<head>
<script type="text/javascript">
function startTime() {
    var today = new Date();
    var h = today.getHours();
    var m = today.getMinutes();
    var s = today.getSeconds();
    // add a zero in front of numbers<10
    m = checkTime(m);
    s = checkTime(s);
    document.getElementById('txt').innerHTML  =  h  +
":" + m + ":" + s;
    t = setTimeout('startTime()', 500);
}

function checkTime(i) {
    if (i < 10) {
        i = "0" + i;
    }
    return i;
}
</script>
</head>

<body onload="startTime()">
```

```
<div id="txt"></div>
</body>
</html>
```

In this chapter we learned how to make a function and to call a function for our suitability. Functions prove to be very useful as they can be reused as many times as we want.

Chapter 7: Arrays

Arrays are special variables used for holding more than one value at a time. If you have a list of items, for example car names, storing the cars in single variable could look like this:

```
var cara = "Saab";
var carb = "Volvo";
var carc = "BMW";
```

What if you want to loop through the cars and find a particular one? What if have 300 cars, not just 3? It would be hard to create and keep track of that many individual variables. In these type of situations the array is the solution.

An array is capable of holding many values under a single name, and those values can be accessed by referring to an index number.

Creating an Array

An array literal is the easiest way of creating a JavaScript Array.

Syntax:

```
var array-name = [item1, item2, ...];
```

Example:

```
var cars = ["Saab", "Volvo", "BMW"];
```

The next example also creates an Array as well as assigns values to it.

Example:

```
var cars = new Array("Saab", "Volvo", "BMW");
```

Accessing the Elements of an Array

An array element is referred to by referring to the **index number**. This statement will access the first element value in cars:

```
var name = cars[0];
```

This statement performs the function of modifying the first element in cars:

```
cars[0] = "Porsche";
```

Loops

By using a loop, a block of code can be executed a number of times. Loops prove to be handy if the same code is run over and over again, each time with a different value. This is the case often when working with arrays. Instead of writing:

```
text += cars[0] + "<br>";
text += cars[1] + "<br>";
text += cars[2] + "<br>";
text += cars[3] + "<br>";
text += cars[4] + "<br>";
text += cars[5] + "<br>";
```

You can write:

```
for (i = 0; i < cars.length; i++) {
    text += cars[i] + "<br>";
}
```

Different Kinds of Loops

JavaScript can support different kinds of loops:

for - The for loop will loop through a block of code a number of times

for/in – The for/in loop will loop through the object properties.

while – The while loop will loop through a block of code while a specified condition is true.

do/while – This loop also loops through a block of code while a specified condition is true.

The For Loop

The for loop is the go to tool that you will use when you want to create a loop. It has the following syntax:

```
for (statement a; statement b; statement c) {
    code block to be executed
}
```

Statement a is executed before the loop, or the code block, starts.

Statement b defines the condition for running the loop and executing the code block.

Statement c is executed each time after the loop (the code block) has been executed.

Example:

```
for (i = 0; i < 5; i++) {
    text += "The number is " + i + "<br>";
}
```


From the above example, you may read:

Statement a sets a variable before the loop starts (var i = 0).

Statement b defines the condition for the loop to run (i must be less than 5).

Statement c increments the value of i by one (i++) each time the code block in the loop has been executed.

Statement a

Normally you will use statement a to initiate the variable used in the loop (var i = 0). This is not always the case -- JavaScript doesn't care. Statement a is optional. You can initiate many values in statement a (separated by comma):

Example:

```
for (i = 0, len = cars.length, text = ""; i < len;
i++) {
    text += cars[i] + "<br>";
}
```

You can remove statement a entirely. For example, you might not need it as your values are set before the loop starts.

Example:

```
var i = 2;
var len = cars.length;
var text = "";
for (; i < len; i++) {
    text += cars[i] + "<br>";
}
```

Statement b

Often statement b is used to evaluate the condition of the initial variable. This is not always the case. Again, JavaScript doesn't care. Statement b is also optional. If statement b returns true, the loop will start over again, if it returns false, the loop will end.

Statement c

Often statement c increments the initial variable. This is not always the case, but it is a common pattern. Statement c is also optional. Statement c can do anything like decrement (i--), perform a larger increment (i = i + 15), or do anything else, for that matter.

Statement c can also be omitted (like when you increment your values inside the loop):

Example:

```
var i = 0
var len = cars.length;
for (; i < len;) {
    text += cars[i] + "<br>";
    i++;
}
```

The For/In Loop

The for/in statement loops through the properties of an object.

Example:

```
var person = {
    fname: "John",
    lname: "Doe",
    age: 25
};
var text = "";
var x;
for (x in person) {
    text += person[x];
}
```

While Loop

The while loop executes a code block as long as the specified condition is true.

Syntax:

```
while (condition) {
    code block to be executed
}
```

Example:

In the next example, the code in the loop will run again and again as long as a variable (i) is less than 10.

```
while (i < 10) {
    text += "The number is " + i;
    i++;
}
```

Do/While Loop

This loop is a variant of the while loop. It executes the code block once before checking whether the condition is true. It then continues to repeat while the condition is true.

Syntax:

```
do {
    code block to be executed
}
while (condition);
```

Example:

The next example uses a do/while loop. The loop executes at least once, even though the condition is false, as the code block is executed before the condition is tested.

```
var i = 20
do {
    text += "The number is " + i;
    i++;
}
while (i < 10);
```

Comparing the For and While Loops

A while loop is almost the same as a for loop with statement a and statement c omitted. The loop in the given example uses a while loop for the collection of car names from the cars array.

Example:

```
cars = ["BMW", "Volvo", "Saab", "Ford"];
var i = 0;
var text = "";
while (cars[i]) {
    text += cars[i] + "<br>";
    i++;
}
```

A block of code will be executed by the loop as long as the given condition is true.

The Do/While Loop

This loop is a variant of the while loop. It executes the code block once before checking whether the condition is true. It then repeats the loop as long as the condition is true.

Syntax:

```
do {
    code block to be executed
}
while (condition);
```

Example:

The next example will use a do/while loop. The loop is always executed at least once even when the condition is false as the code block is executed before the condition is tested.

```
do {
    text += "The number is " + i;
    i++;
}
while (i < 10);
```

Remeber to increase the variable used in the condition or the loop will never end!

Comparing the For and While Loops

A while loop is almost the same as a for loop, with statement a and statement c omitted. The loop in the next example will use a **for loop** on the collection of the car names that are in the cars array.

Example:

```
cars = ["BMW", "Volvo", "Saab", "Ford"];
var i = 0;
```

```
var text = "";
for (; cars[i];) {
    text += cars[i] + "<br>";
    i++;
}
```

The loop in this example uses a while loop to collect car names from the cars array.

```
cars = ["BMW", "Volvo", "Saab", "Ford"];
var i = 0;
var text = "";
while (cars[i]) {
    text += cars[i] + "<br>";
    i++;
}
```

Chapter 8: Associative Arrays

Imagine you have a mouseover / click image swap script. Suppose want to keep track of the status of each image, be it normal, clicked or mouseovered. Additionally you want to be able to access the status by image name. Therefore if you have an image which is named '*Home*' you want to be able query it's status and get a return value of normal, mouseovered, or clicked. To do this you will need to use JavaScript objects. It will look like this:

```
theStatus.Home
```

JavaScript Objects

JavaScript is an object oriented language. In practice the objects that are defined by the programmer himself are used less, except in complex DOM API's. The standard objects such as document and window and their many offspring are very necessary, but the browser defines them, not the programmer.

Methods and Properties

You can define your own objects in Javascript. Additionally, you may assign methods and properties to each of them, be they self-defined or prewritten.

Methods in Javascript are things that do something, and you can recognize them by their parenthesis () . When they are called they perform a certain action and optionally returns a value.

Properties in Javascript are like variables that hold values and when queried, returns those values. The values they can hold include numbers, strings or a Boolean value. When they are called, we get a value.

JavaScript functions are also methods, hence the parenthesis.

```
document.write('text');
```

When you perform the above example, you are executing the pre-defined write() method of the document object. When you are writing your own functions you are adding methods to the window object, which is the parent of all other JavaScript objects.

Similarly, when you ask for the innerHeight of a page, you are accessing a property of the window object. If you are defining a variable of your own, a new property to the window object is added by you.

You already use properties and methods in everyday

JavaScripting. As most of these are preprogrammed variables and functions, you mostly don't need to worry about the objects themselves as they're "black boxes" that you can use without concerning yourself of the details of how they are implemented. The properties and methods (variables and functions) that are defined yourself are almost always added to the window object.

How to Define an Object and Properties

Here is how we can create an object of our own.

```
var theStatus = new Object;
```

We have now initialized our theStatus object and we can start adding properties. In this example we want to create one property for every image on the page. Here is one way we can do this.

```
theStatus.Home = 'normal';
```

We have now added a new property Home to the object and we set its value to the string "normal". JavaScript is case sensitive, therefore the property home will not exist, only Home.

This is very useful, but while using this notation we will face problems later on if we want to make a property of theStatus for every image on the page. The property must have the similar name as the image and it should have a 'normal' value . We cannot do:

```
var x = document.images;
for (var i = 0; i < x.length; i++) {
    var theName = x[i].name;
    theStatus.theName = 'normal';
}
```

We will now pick the name from each image and will create a new property with the same name.

```
theStatus.theName = 'normal';
```

With the execution of the above line of code JS- creates a new property, theName and set its value to normal. So in the end we are left with one property, theName.

Associative Arrays

Objects are also associative arrays, sometimes called hashes, in Javascript. This means, the property theStatus.Home can be written or read by calling theStatus['Home'].

You can therefore access every property by entering the property name as a string into this array. This type of array will associate every key with a value and here the key Home is associated with the value normal. It is also called a hash in the Perl programming language. Unlike Perl, JavaScript will automatically create an associative array for every object. You may see such behaviour with common objects in a form, for example. A form can be accessed by performing either of these DOM calls:

```
document.forms['theForm']
document.forms.theForm
```

You may also use document.theForm, but that will be a special case, and not a regular behaviour of JavaScript associative/object arrays. Therefore if we want to set the status of an image to 'normal' in our object, we can do the following and it will work.

```
var x = document.images;
for (var i = 0; i < x.length; i++) {
    var theName = x[i].name;
    theStatus[theName] = 'normal';
}
```

We now put theName, which is a string, into the brackets [] where a string is expected. Therefore you make a new key/value pair which will be the same as a new property with a value. Basically you have the power to let one name or string refer to another one.

Accessing Each Element in an Associative Array

The for (var in object) pattern is equivalent to Perl's foreach $key (keys %hash). You can go through each element of a normal array by by doing the following.

```
var x = [the array];
for (var i = 0; i < x.length; i++) {
    do something with x[i]
}
```

You may also go through every element of an associative array. Let's say you want to go through the status values of all the images. If the image has the status 'mouseover' you want to call a function callFn() and pass the image name to it. You can do it like this:

```
if (theStatus.Home == 'mouseover') callFn('Home');
if (theStatus.Place == 'mouseover') callFn('Place');
// etc.
```

Or:

```
if (theStatus['Home'] == 'mouseover') callFn('Home');
if (theStatus['Place'] == 'mouseover') callFn('Place');
// etc
```

Doing it this way will quickly will lead to immense scripts. Additionally, if you rename an image later on you also need to change a line of code and if you forget, you get errors. This is obviously less than ideal. JavaScript has the for/in statement which is exactly perfect for this situation.

```
for (var i in theStatus) {
    if (theStatus[i] == 'mouseover') callFn(i);
}
```

You will go through all properties of the theStatus object (all keys in the associative array theStatus). The variable i will succesively become each property name of the object. This way you can do something with theStatus[i] and it will be done to each property. If the value of the image status is 'mouseover' you call callFn() and pass it the key.

JavaScript does not guarantee any specific order for the properties.

Other Books by the Author

C# Programming for Beginners
http://www.linuxtrainingacademy.com/c-sharp

C# is a simple and general-purpose object-oriented programming language. Combine this with its versatility and huge standard library it's easy to see why it's such a popular and well-respected programming language.

When you learn how to program in C# you will be able to develop web based applications or graphical desktop applications. One of the best things about C# is that it's easy to learn... especially with this book.

Scrum Essentials
http://www.linuxtrainingacademy.com/scrum-book

You have a limited amount of time to create software, especially when you're given a deadline, self-imposed or not. You'll want to make sure that the software you build is at least decent but more importantly, on time. How do you balance quality with time? This book dives into these very important topics. After reading *Scrum Essentials* you will know all about scrum roles, sprints, scrum artifacts, and much more.

Java Programming
http://www.linuxtrainingacademy.com/java-programming

Java is one of the most widely used and powerful computer programming languages in existence today. Once you learn how to program in Java you can create software applications that run on servers, desktop computers, tablets, phones, Blu-ray players, and more.

Also, if you want to ensure your software behaves the same regardless of which operation system it runs on, then Java's "write once, run anywhere" philosophy is for you. Java was design to be platform independent allowing you to create applications that run on a variety of operating systems including Windows, Mac, Solaris, and Linux.

Additional Resources

Common Coding Problems Solved Using JavaScript
http://www.linuxtrainingacademy.com/javascript-guide/

As a thank you for reading this book, I would like to give you a free copy of "Common Coding Problems Solved Using JavaScript." It's a perfect complement to this book and will help you along your JavaScript journey.

Create Your Own Programming Language
http://linuxtrainingacademy.com/create-your-own-language

A System To Achieve Every Programmer's Dream. Learn How To Create A Simple Programming Language In A Few Days With This Easy Step-by-step Guide

Learn Programming: from Novice to JavaScript Guru in 2 Weeks
http://www.linuxtrainingacademy.com/javascript-guru

This video training course is a step-by-step guide with all the tools and resources you need to master all your web projects with ease and confidence.

Learning JavaScript Programming Tutorial: A Definitive Guide
http://www.linuxtrainingacademy.com/javascript-definitive

In this training course you will learn the basics of programming with JavaScript, the worlds most used programming language. The tutorial is designed for the absolute beginner - no prior JavaScript programming experience is required in order to get the most out of this video training.

The Ultimate Guide To Node.js + Express
http://www.linuxtrainingacademy.com/nodejs-express

Learn all you need to know about programming with Node and Express so you can build a JavaScript web app quickly.

Appendix

Appendix A: Trademarks

JavaScript is a trademark of Oracle Corporation.
Linux® is the registered trademark of Linus Torvalds in the U.S.
and other countries.
Mac and OS X are trademarks of Apple Inc., registered in the U.S.
and other countries.
Open Source is a registered certification mark of Open Source
Initiative.
UNIX is a registered trademark of The Open Group.
Windows is a registered trademark of Microsoft Corporation in
the United States and other countries.
All other product names mentioned herein are the trademarks of
their respective owners.

www.ingramcontent.com/pod-product-compliance
Lightning Source LLC
Chambersburg PA
CBHW071010050326

40689CB00014B/3564